WHAT'S IT ALL ABOUT?

Rev. George W. Kosicki, C.S.B.

WHAT'S IT ALL ABOUT

Letters of
Reflection
on Human
Freedom,
Mercy
And
Humility

Rev. George W. Kosicki, C.S.B.

FAITH PUBLISHING COMPANY
P.O. Box 237
Milford, OH 45150

Published by Faith Publishing Company

For additional copies write:

> Faith Publishing Company
> P.O. Box 237
> Milford, Ohio 45150

Contents

Dedication

To Bob, Maureen, and Bobbie Digan who have offered their lives that God's mercy may be proclaimed, and to whom these meditations were originally sent.

G.W.K.

Foreword

As He began His public ministry, the first "homily" of Jesus Christ was rather brief. He stated:

> "The Kingdom of God is at hand. Reform your lives and believe in the gospel." (*Mk.* 1:15).

Rather short, but certainly to the point! It appears however, that mankind never really got it, for the same question has been re-surfacing ever since: "What's it all about?"

In the process, through the centuries, we have continued to ponder the mysteries of life, of soul, of eternal life hereafter, struggling to grasp hold of the elements of grace, faith, spirituality, while trying to cast aside the dark shadow of sin, despair, frustration.

Through a series of meditations, written in letter form to a family of close friendship, Fr. George Kosicki provides us with some excellent insights in answer to that age old question. His thoughts, as well as his directions, are straightforward, to the point, and reflect a confirmation of the truths we have long recognized in the Bible, but seldom follow through on. Fr. George's meditations require the same input from us the reader, namely, "meditation." In doing so, we can get beyond the problem of hearing or reading something we don't want to accept, and zero in on "The way, the truth, and the life" instead.

Fr. George recognizes the need for "forgiveness and mercy" as two key ingredients for successfully living out the answer to that question. They are ingredients that are largely abandoned in our whirlwind society of today. Additionally, Fr. George takes us deeper into the mystery of the Eucharist, and through it, the bonding to Jesus Christ, that special gift of "Flesh of My flesh," emerges.

In WHAT'S IT ALL ABOUT, the author provides us with a capsule summary of the whole question, laced with insights toward those elements which raise mankind above the human plane. For it is only there that the answer has meaning.

Faith Publishing Company

1. "This Year the Earth Spoke. . ."

January 1, 1989

May the Lord bless you with His peace in the New Year and Mary, our mother, care for you. What's it all about?

This is a question that can come to our minds so easily these days. What is this life about? What is its meaning, its purpose, its value? These questions arise from within as we observe the situation in the world around us and as we see in our church as well.

Time magazine has just come out with a new approach. They did not choose a "man of the year" but instead chose the "Planet of the Year; The Endangered Earth" (Jan. 2, 1989). A startling caption caught my attention: "This year the earth spoke, like God warning Noah of the deluge, and people began to listen."

My thoughts flashed to the encyclical of Pope John Paul II, *Dives in Misericordia (Rich in Mercy)*. In the concluding chapter he appeals to the church to cry out for mercy on this world:

"and like prophets, let us appeal to that love which has maternal characteristics— and which like a mother goes after each of her children, after each lost sheep, even

if the lost are in the millions, *even if mankind earns by its sin a kind of modern
'flood', as did the generation of Noah"*
(emphasis added).

Yes, the earth is endangered because of the
sin of man. The consequences of abusing our
freedom are crying out: pollution, depletion of
natural resources, toxic wastes. As a consequence
the earth is speaking with loud cries: floods,
earthquakes, fires, hurricanes, drought, and man
is suffering tragic deaths, poverty and starvation.
All these echo the sins of man—injustice, avarice, pride, anger, revenge, lust for power.

The *Time* magazine articles give practical suggestions on "What Nations Should Do," even
printing them in bold colored side-bars. The suggestions are well thought out by a team of top
experts from around the world and were
presented to the Time Magazine Environment
Conference (November '88, Boulder, Colorado).
These suggestions can be effective and should
be agreed upon by the nations and carried out.
But, there is more that needs to be done to answer the real needs of man that has brought on
these consequences upon his home planet earth.
Time magazine deals only with the consequences of man's ignorance and careless actions
and does not deal with the real problem. The
real problem is man's SIN! We have abused our
freedom by the practical rejection of God's
dominion over our lives. The greatest sin is the
continued rebellious independence from God.

In violating his freedom man is also violating mother earth.

The response to the out cry of mother earth begins with our repentance, our turning from sin and turning to the living God with trust, asking for his mercy on us and on the whole world.

2. Why the Turmoil? The Black Cloud

January 2, 1989

May the Lord bless you with His peace and presence.

The other day I concelebrated at a funeral Mass of a priest confrere of mine; a most gentle and gracious man who reached out with love to all he met. He took on the sufferings of those around him and brought healing with his love. So many experienced his compassion as testified by various people at the funeral and by a packed church at the Mass. Some sixty priests concelebrated with the bishop. The bishop gave a powerful homily on the transforming power of suffering.

And yet I was under a black cloud, attacked as it were by my resentments and judgments of the local ordinary because of his public statements and attitudes. I cried out in my heart for mercy for him and for myself, for compassion, for understanding for my critical thoughts of the way he interpreted the rubrics of the consecration of the Mass. Lord, spare me from myself! What's it all about?

Yes, what is it all about? What is going on when we find ourselves in these "black cloud" situations? What is real and what is only in me? Over the years I've tried to gain some wisdom on how to deal with the black cloud syndrome but they haven't disappeared!

In simple faith and trust I've tried to intercede for people in this situation. The black cloud is a burden of interior suffering—a pain of the heart—that cries out for mercy. "Jesus, have mercy on us and on the whole world." The presence of the black cloud is a continual reminder to pray for mercy. If I weren't aware of the black cloud I wouldn't remember to pray for mercy.

Unfortunately, this approach doesn't take away the pain of the heart. It does, however, give some meaning to it and so in simple trust I continue to cry "Jesus Mercy."

Another awareness also helps in these situations. The Lord has created us free and wants us to exercise that freedom in accordance with His will. He so respects the freedom of His creatures that He will not violate their exercise of freedom. Who am I not to imitate God? Am I not to respect the freedom of my brothers and sisters, even as God respects my freedom?

And yet there is real and objective abuse and violation of our freedom in rejecting God's authority and the legitimate authority of the Church established by Him. Who is to be the judge of this violation? Am I? Is my black cloud experience a sign that I should judge and condemn? Am I to shut my eyes to the real situation?

What is it all about? Real, objective, evil and sin do in fact exist in the Church and world. Am I supposed to do something about it? Yes.

I am to see and to feel the pain of the situation. But I am not to judge with condemnation, rather it may be said that I am to judge with mercy. Above all we must cry out for mercy and be merciful to the extent we are able and are responsible for the situation.

The problem of sin and evil, both objective and subjective, is a great mystery, a mystery like a great black cloud, rather like the darkness that covered the whole land during the crucifixion of Christ (*Mt.* 27:45). Only the power of the Holy Spirit that raised Jesus from the dead can break through the black cloud of sin and evil and bring us the light of resurrection.

During the funeral, as I stood right next to the body of my brother priest throughout the Mass, I asked the Lord for the grace of His compassion for all people. I continue to ask for that special grace to radiate the Lord's mercy, because I so need it.

Lord help me to walk in humility, trusting and rejoicing.

3. God Respects Our Freedom

January 3, 1989

Peace!

What a God we have! He respects our freedom even to the point of allowing us to sin and abuse our freedom and so cause suffering. He wants us to use our freedom in order to freely seek Him and to submit to Him. He will even allow us to stumble along our way and fall flat on our faces. Yet He continues to call us, to pursue us and reach out to us that we might freely follow Him—even when we are attacked by a black cloud!

This is the way Jesus dealt with the twelve apostles which He Himself chose and called. None of them were saints to start with. Peter was a braggart. John and James were revengeful. Simon was a political extremist. Thomas was a doubter. Judas betrayed Him and they all left Him in the garden of Gesthemani. Yet Jesus respected the men He called. He drew them on to holiness and reprimanded them when needed, corrected and taught them, but above all prayed for them and respected their freedom and their place in their spiritual journey.

Why is it that God respects our freedom? It

7

seems to me that He sees in us what He created, namely, His own image and likeness. He sees what can be and will be if we freely cooperate and continue on the journey. The Father wants to make more sons and daughters like Jesus— faithful, obedient, humble, in the very image of Jesus.

The key to grasping God's plan is *humility.* It is because of His humility that He respects our freedom. God is so humble that He will not violate our freedom. Rather He patiently waits and pursues us that we might respond to His merciful love.

The description of the Lord standing at the door of our hearts and knocking (*cf. Revelation* 3:20) is the most powerful picture of humility I know of. God stands and waits! He waits for us to freely open the door of our hearts so that He could enter and sup with us in communion. How humble can God get!?

Who am I not to imitate the Lord? In the midst of the black cloud syndrome am I to judge and condemn? Am I to violate my brother's freedom, even if he stumbles? Am I to curse him and make the black cloud even darker?

The example of the humility of Jesus exhorts and urges me to humility, to patience and to cry for mercy that my brother may move even closer, even freer in Christ Jesus.

None of us are in the same place in our journey. None of us know how the Lord is working in the hearts of our brothers or sisters. The popular poster says this well: "Be patient. God is not finished with me yet."

When we do see and encounter sin and evil, we need to respond with the humility and mercy of Jesus—that humility and mercy is what the crucifixion of Jesus is about. It is that humility and mercy that brought us salvation from sin and evil—at the price of suffering offered with love. Our confrontation with sin and evil will also cause us suffering and pain, and the black cloud will come upon us. But offered with love in union with Jesus, it brings redemption. Our suffering offered with love is redeeming.

When we are humble and merciful, we too will obtain mercy like Jesus. Like Jesus, we too will experience resurrection, the fullness of mercy and be a source of mercy to those in need.

And what a gift we have in the Sacrament of Reconciliation! We can confess our sins of judgment committed under the black cloud. In this "tribunal of mercy" we receive mercy i.e. the forgiveness of sin. By humbling ourselves we receive mercy not only for ourselves but for all those in need, for all those we see trapped in sin and evil. In this way the pain and suffering of our black cloud becomes the occasion and vehicle for mercy on us and on the whole world.

What's it all about? Why this suffering? Why this humility? Because God is love, He is also humble. And because of this love He suffers. In His humility, He so respects our freedom which He created, that He will not violate it.

And so what's it all about? Freedom! God, waiting for us to freely submit, stands at the door of our hearts, knocking and waiting for us to open up to Him freely and say "Come, Lord Jesus! That is humility!

4. But There Is Real Sin And Evil!

January 4, 1989

May the merciful Lord fill you with His peace.

How are we to respond to real sin and evil around us? We cannot deny it because it is so obvious; nor can we hide our heads in the sand and say it doesn't exist because we don't see it. Nor can we remedy every situation by our own efforts.

But there are certain things we can do about tragedies like the explosion of the Pan Am flight 103, about the tensions in the mid-east, about the drug abuse problems, about abortion and the many, many evils around us. We can suffer in solidarity with those in pain. We can cry out "Have Mercy on us and on the whole world." We can do even more by dealing with the real roots of the problem in our own hearts, that is, the sin in our lives. Anger, avarice, pride are always there to repent of and do reparation for.

I've been listening to a tape of Father Henri Nouwen (*"Desert Spirituality and Contemporary Ministry"*), on the effect of solitude. He confirmed something I was beginning to be more and more aware of as a result of my own solitude and that is the growing consciousness of

my own sinfulness and at the same time a growing awareness of the effect of sin on others. There
is a solidarity in sin, and all of us are responsible
because of our own sin. But also there is a solidarity in redemption, and we can help each other
and those in misery by our compassion. The effect of solitude is to face up to the real sin in
our lives and plead for mercy. In a sense we "die
to our neighbor," because we can no longer see
his sin and judge with condemnation, but only
judge with mercy, with compassion. We suffer
with him in the solidarity of our pain and cry
"Mercy." In solitude we become aware of the
dead person in our own house, and we grow
in compassion. It is a time of spiritual warfare.

Father Nouwen's main theme in these tapes
and in his recent writing is solitude, silence, and
prayer, as a remedy for the mad rush of the modern secular society. We need to retreat into the
solitude of the desert of our hearts. There we
encounter our own sin, misery, darkness and pain
and grow in compassion. Each day we need to
take the time to flee to the desert of our hearts
and adore the living God Who dwells within us.
Here we will give birth to compassion. Here we
will cry out in solidarity for mercy.

The little bit that we can do in response to
the real sin and evil of the world becomes in-
finitely multiplied by the compassion of the Lord
Himself. His compassion is greater than all our
sin, all our evil, all our misery, greater than all
the sin and misery of the world combined. But

we must *ask* for His mercy in order to exercise the freedom He has given us by asking.

This way of responding is a humble way but humility is the key to the power of God. Our humility draws down the mighty mercy of God. The humble way of solitude, silence, and prayer draws down mercy on us and on the whole world.

What is it all about? It is the humble exercise of our free will. In submitting our own repentance and pain in solidarity with the pain of the world, we enter into the great act of the Eucharist and consecrate the world to the Father (cf. *Lumen Gentium,* 34).

The current teaching of Father Nouwen, that solitude gives birth to compassion, is the teaching of the desert fathers, like Saint Anthony of the desert. It also confirms what has been happening in my own life. It was in solitude with the Camalodese hermits that I was first drawn to work in the apostolate of Divine Mercy and went to Stockbridge, Massachusettes for three months of study. Then again, in the hermitage I was drawn to devote my life to proclaiming God's mercy, first as director of the Divine Mercy Department and now after a third period of solitude, I am in the midst of setting up a foundation of Divine Mercy. The fundamental insight into this present ministry is to spend half the time in solitude and out of that solitude, prayer to proclaim God's mercy to those in need. Solitude has given birth to mercy.

I want to confirm the insight of Father Nouwen that the root of ministry is in solitude. In solitude we find the root of sin and evil in our heart and grow in compassion.

5. Souls, Souls, Give Me Souls

January 5, 1989

May the merciful Lord bless you with His love and presence.

What's it all about? All the struggle and pain of life! What's life all about?

In my thinking it comes down to the face to face encounter of our freedom and God's. God in His freedom and love has created us to share in His freedom in order that we can freely choose to love Him. It is a confrontation of God and the soul. Here, I am using the word "soul" as the whole human person, as unique and alive. The victory in this encounter is submission to God's freedom and His will. The battle of life is over our free will surrendering: are we willing to freely exercise our free will and say "yes" to God?

This surrender to the will of God is a continuous act of faith, of trust, of love, and of adoration. By this act we freely acknowledge God's existence, His dominion and care of us, and His love for us. It is in this act of surrender that we receive His loving mercy. From God's point of view this capturing of souls with His love is His plan for us, and His greatest desire. What He has in store for us is beyond all our dreams:

> "Eye has not seen, ear has not heard,
> nor has it so much as dawned on man,
> what God has prepared for those who
> love Him" (*1 Cor.* 2:9).

But this same plan of love, freely given, has God in what I call a "dilemma." On the one hand God is in love with us and would love to possess us, but on the other hand that would violate our freedom. So the Lord like a frustrated lover, hovers over us waiting, sometimes not so patiently, until we open our hearts with a freely given "yes" to Him. He really does stand at the door of our hearts and knocks until we open up to Him (cf. *Rev.* 3:20). He stands and waits in utter humility, because He is so humble that He respects our freedom.

The Lord has expressed to various mystics His desire for souls. This is the way Our Lord expressed longing to Sister Faustina:

> I want to give Myself to souls; I yearn
> for souls (*Diary* 206).

> I thirst. I thirst for the salvation of
> souls. Help Me, My daughter, to save souls.
> Join your suffering to My passion and
> offer them to the heavenly Father for sinners (*Diary* 1032).

> My daughter give Me souls. Know that
> it is your mission to *win souls* for Me

by prayer and sacrifice. How very much
I desire the salvation of souls! My dearest
secretary, write that I want to pour out
My divine life into human souls and to
sanctify them, *if only they were willing
to accept My grace.* The greatest sinners
would achieve great sanctity, *if only they
would trust in My mercy.* . . (*Diary*
1784).

"If only. . ." if only they were willing, if only
they would trust, if only they would accept, if
only they would exercise their great gift of freedom, if only they would surrender to His merciful love, if only they knew the gift of God (cf.
Jn. 4:10). "If only" is the very touch point of
man and God—if only he would use his free will
to freely respond and cooperate with God's will
and not his own.

What's it all about? From God's point of view
it's about this "if only!" God is waiting with
love for our fiat, our yes to His word (cf. *Lk.*
1:38). He asks for and waits for our cooperation
not only for the salvation and sanctification of
our own souls, but even more, marvelous to say,
He wants our cooperation to save and sanctify
the souls of others!

To Sister Faustina the Lord points out her mis-
sion in life is to use her freedom to win souls.
By the exercise of her free will in prayer, offer-
ing of her sufferings, and encouraging others to
trust in God's mercy, she cooperated in the victory of winning souls for God. What a magnifi-

cent vocation! And this vocation is for you and me, *if only*, we say "yes" to the Father's plan of mercy.

Let us ask God for the grace to trust Him more deeply, to cooperate with His plan for the salvation and sanctification of souls.

6. Extreme Humility

May the merciful Lord fill you with His peace and mercy.

In front of me on my desk is the photograph of "The extreme humility" which I received as a gift last Christmas. It is there as a reminder of the humility of Jesus. It is a presence of the humble Jesus who not only became man but was crucified and buried in a tomb for our salvation and sanctification. This icon, honored by the Byzantine church on Holy Saturday, depicts the torso of the crucified Jesus standing in the tomb against the background of the cross. The wounds in His hands and side are visible. The iconographer, George Boganopolis, of Patras, Greece, portrayed this icon on a circular medallion, expressing the totality of Christ's emptying of Himself. It is a visual presence of the hymn from St. Paul's letter to the Philippians:

> Have among yourselves the same attitude that is in Christ Jesus, Who, though He was in the form of God, did not regard equality with God something to be grasped. Rather, He emptied Himself, taking the form of a slave, coming in human

likeness, and found human in appearance,
He humbled Himself, becoming obedient
to death, even death on a cross. . . (*Phil*
2:5-8).

"Though He was in the form of God" can also
be translated from the Greek as "*because* He was
in the form of God." It is *because* He is God
that He humbled Himself, not despite the fact
that He is God.

By His very nature God is humble. We can
know something of who God is, by the way He
acts and operates. He acted in this extremely humble way because He is humility itself. His humble nature is seen in the different way in which
He treats the humble and the proud:

He has shown might with His arms, dis-
persed the arrogant of mind and heart.
He has thrown down the rulers from
their thrones but lifted up the lowly.
The hungry He has filled with good
things; the rich He has sent away empty
(*Lk.* 1:51-53).

God deposes the proud and exalts the humble, because He acts according to His nature. He
acts humbly because He is humble. By His very
nature He has to depose the proud and fill the
lowly with mercy.

The nature of God's humility became more
clear to me during the time of solitude this past
fall with the Camalodese hermits. The nature of

God's humility is seen in its totality—total giving and total receiving. Pope Paul VI uses a joyful expression to describe this total giving and receiving as the "secret of the Trinity:"

> The Father is seen here as the one Who gives Himself to the Son, without reserve and without ceasing, in a burst of joyful generosity; and the Son is seen as He Who gives Himself in the same way to the Father, in a burst of joyful gratitude, in the Holy Spirit (Paul VI, *Gaudete in Domino*).

This infinite circle of love which includes justice, sets in motion mercy (cf. John Paul II, *Dives in Misericordia*). It extends that love to us in creation and then in redemption. This love poured out on us as sinners is *mercy*. This great mercy totally given in Christ Jesus is also totally received by Jesus in His resurrection (cf. *Dives in Misericordia*). Jesus totally fulfilled the beatitude:

> Blessed are the merciful, for they shall obtain mercy (*Mt.* 5:7).

This great circle of mercy is simultaneously the great circle of humility—total receiving, total giving. Only the humble are capable of receiving God's mercy. Because of His extreme humility, Christ received "mercy," that is, He received from the Father resurrection and the proclamation of Lord in the totality of His humanity, as well as His divinity. In this light the continuation of the hymn of St. Paul to the Philippians takes on a richer meaning:

> Because of this, God greatly exalted Him and bestowed on Him the name that is above every name, that at the name of Jesus every knee should bend, of those in Heaven and on earth and under the earth, and every tongue confess that Jesus Christ is Lord, to the glory of God the Father (*Phil* 2:9-11).

Because of His humility, the name given to Jesus is *LORD*!

Again we hear St. Peter on the day of Pentecost, concluding his preaching with this same proclamation of Jesus as Lord because of his humility:

> Therefore let the whole house of Israel know for certain that God has made Him Lord and Messiah, this Jesus Whom you crucified (*Acts* 2:36).

So what's it all about? It's about entering into the great circle of mercy and humility, so that we may be saved from sin and evil and be sanctified as children of God. We enter into this circle of salvation and sanctification by baptism. We enter into the death of Jesus so that we may share in His resurrection. Baptism is only the birth, only the beginning of our new life. We continue to grow and mature as we enter more fully into the circle of mercy and humility.

There are a number of ways to enter more fully into this great circle of God's love poured out upon us sinners. Let this be a topic of another letter.

Today, I want to thank God for His extreme humility and extreme mercy.

7. A Plurality of Infallibility

January 7, 1989

May the merciful Lord fill you with His joy.

Yesterday, I read an article by a fellow Basilian, Father Michael Miller, C.S.B., *Catholics against the Pope: The anti-Roman Complex in America* (Canadian Catholic Review, January, 1989). He describes the growth of an "American" Church where the papacy would be accommodated to the American experience, documenting the complaints against the Papal ministry and against John Paul II. He compares the progressive steps of criticism and attacks to that of Martin Luther whose last will and testament to his followers was unequivocal: "Preserve this one thing when I am dead: hatred of the Roman pontiff." Father Miller asks if we are on the brink of a new Reformation? He prays not, but the similarity between the Reformers, and the Americanists' understanding of the papacy is cause for alarm.

This article stirred me to write on the question of the many and growing number of teachers and writers who in effect consider their position as correct even infallible. This I call a "plurality of infallibility." This title I've saved for several years because I wanted to write an article about the situation. It seemed to me that the title alone was enough to carry the message without further explanation. Now I see that some reflection is needed. How easily we consider ourselves "infallible" in our judgments.

The issue of plurality of infallibility has to do with humility and submission—two unpopular virtues in our democratic America where the subject of fredom is such a battle cry. It seems that the "spirit of '76," which characterized the fighters of the American revolutionary war is now a characteristic of the American Church. There is today an attitude of rebellious independence, demanding our rights and freedom and participation in all the decision making as though the Church were a democracy. However, the Church is not a democracy for the people, by the people, but a theocracy. It is God's Church, not mine. It is for His glory, not mine. Christ appointed ONE man to be His vicar on earth, guiding us in faith and morals in an infallible way. Now, it seems, we have a growing number of "popes."

The true use of our freedom is not to choose our independence, but rather to freely choose our dependence on God. In God alone we find our true freedom. He is the source and goal of our life and freedom:

> If you remain in My word, you will truly be My disciples, and you will know the truth, and the truth will set you free. . . . If the Son sets you free, then you will truly be free (*Jn.* 8:32-36).

God created us in His own image and likeness (cf. *Gen.* 1:26), to share in His dominion
through the gift of freedom and the power of
reasoning. These gifts from God are intended
to be received, used, and developed in ways
that will honor God. All gifts are to be returned
to God with thanksgiving. When this freedom
and reason is turned in on ourself, it is an abuse
of the gifts of God and a distortion of our image
and likeness of God.

The rebellion and criticism against the office
and person of the pope is a blatant manifesta-
tion of the abuse of our freedom. The consequences of such actions will be devastating to
the Church. I feel that it calls for intercessory
prayer, pleading for the mercy of God to inter-
vene. I feel that the situation is beyond arguments
and polemics. Now is the time for God's sover-
eign action.

It is for this reason that I look forward to the
two months coming up, living right in the Vatican City at the Teutonic College, where I can
pray for God's mercy on us and on the whole
world. What an opportunity to pray for the Holy
Father and the Curia that assist Him. What an
opportunity to translate all he said about God's
mercy into an ardent plea for mercy on the people of the modern world with all their needs
and threats (cf. *Dives in Misericordia,* 15). What
an opportunity to pray for unity, uniting my
prayer with the very prayer of Jesus at the Last
Supper (*Jn.* 7:21), when He prayed for unity. We

need His prayer for unity answered now, more than ever, because now the visible sign of unity, His vicar on earth, Pope John Paul II, is being attacked by those who want a "plurality of infallibility." Join me in Christ's prayer for unity.

8. Your Will Be Done

January 10, 1989

Peace of the Lord be with you.

What's it all about?
Doing God's will!
Doing God's will is another way of expressing our free will, another way of acting in humility. Doing God's will is expressing the truth, the truth that God is God and creator, and we are human beings created by God and we need Him.

"Your will be done" is the very touch point of what it's all about. Our desire is freely expressed in wanting to do God's will, even if we don't know the details of what His will is for this moment and circumstance. The very desire to do God's will already fulfills it. The Lord seems to keep us in the dark about details of His will so that we can walk in faith and continually walk in humility, seeking Him with our whole heart. In this way we freely exercise trust in Him. To trust Him is His great desire for us—this is His will.

St. Augustine said that our whole faith is expressed in the Our Father prayer. It is the prayer that sums up the answers to the question— "What's it all about?" It's about the *kingdom of God,* where Jesus reigns as Lord by the power of the Holy Spirit and to the glory of the Father, both on earth in the hearts of people, as he already reigns in Heaven. This is God's will! We have the blueprint to the fulfillment of God's will in Heaven. Now, His will is that it be accomplished on earth and in our hearts. How? By *trust* and *mercy*! We need to trust Him for our daily bread and be merciful to each other, as He is, and to forgive one another. In this way we will be delivered from the evil one. Truly, His is the kingdom, the power, and the glory, now and forever.

Is it any wonder then that the response of Mary to the plan of God, revealed through the angel Gabriel, was the equivalent of "your will be done": "Behold, I am the handmaid of the Lord. May it be done to me according to your word" (*Lk.* 1:38). This is the response of John the Baptist to the inquiries of his disciples about Jesus: "He must increase; I must decrease" (*Jn.* 3:30). This is the prayer of submission of Jesus to the Father while praying in the garden of Gethsemane: "My Father, if it is possible, let this cup pass from me; yet not as I will but as You will" (*Mt.* 26:39). And again, the purpose of Jesus coming into the world is expressed in the words of Psalm 40: "Behold, I come to do your will, O God" (*Hebrews* 10:7).

Sister Faustina expressed her submission to the will of God in a unique visual way in her diary. On one page she wrote: "From today on, my own will does not exist" and crossed the whole page with a large X. On the next page she wrote only one sentence: "From today on, I do the will of God everywhere, always, and in everything" (*Diary 374*). Submission to the will of God as expressed in obedience to her superiors and spiritual director, was the foundation of her spiritual life. This is what her life was all about—a continual submission to the will of God, a continual act of humility.

Doing God's will and not our own is an act of humility, and is an act that lives out the truth that sets us free. Jesus, by humbly submitting His will to the will of the Father, truly set us free. When we freely and humbly submit to God's will we cooperate with God in this work of setting people free. We are partners in salvation by bringing His mercy to those in need. God asks us to help Him in the salvation of souls—encouraging them to trust and to turn to His mercy. And so we see once again the answer to the question.

What's it all about?

Souls, Souls, salvation of Souls.

9. Humility, Humility, And Again Humility!

January 11, 1989

The merciful Lord bless you with His peace.

What's it all about?
Humility!

Yes, humility is what it is all about. It expresses the free submission to the will of God in a way that is a delight to the Lord. Humility is the foundational virtue on which all the other virtues are built. Humility is THE condition for receiving God's mercy. Humility is the most obvious characteristic of the life of Sister Faustina.

Sister Faustina not only lived a humble life of a servant, working in the kitchen and garden, cleaning the house and answering the door, but more than that she was instructed by her confessor and superiors in the importance of humility.

Father Andrasz, S.J., her confessor, advised her:

> "Humility, humility, and ever humility, as we can do nothing of ourselves. All is purely and simply God's grace" (*Diary* 55).

Mother Mary Joseph her directress in the Novitiate counselled her at the end of the year:

> "Sister, let simplicity and humility be the characteristic traits of your soul. Go through life like a little child, always trusting, always full of simplicity and humility. Content with everything, happy in every circumstance. There, where others fear, you will pass along, thanks to this simplicity and humility. Remember this Sister, for your whole life; as waters flow from the mountains down to the valleys, so too do God's graces flow only into humble souls." (*Diary* 55).

Sister Faustina grew in humility by her child like simplicity and obedience. She also grew in humility by humiliations inflicted by her sisters, at times unknowingly, but at other times maliciously. "Humiliation is my daily food" (*Diary* 92) was her way of expressing it. For example, one day, one of the mothers (probably Mother Jane) poured out so much of her anger upon her, humiliated her so much, that she thought she would not be able to endure it. Mother said to her, "you queer, hysterical visionary, get out of this room! Go on with you!" She continued to pour out her venom. When Sister Faustina returned to her cell, she fell prostrate in silence before the cross. Yet she concealed all this and continued as though nothing happened between them (See *Diary* 128).

The Lord Himself taught Sister Faustina about humility:

> "I keep company with you as a child to teach you humility and simplicity" (*Diary* 184).
>
> "True greatness is in loving God and in humility" (*Diary* 424).
>
> "You are My great joy; your love and your humility make Me leave the heavenly throne and unite Myself with you. Love fills up the abyss that exists between my greatness and your nothingness" (*Diary* 512).
>
> "Know that a pure soul is humble" (*Diary* 576).
>
> "You always please Me by your humility" (*Diary* 1563).
>
> "The torrents of grace inundate humble souls. The proud remain always in poverty and misery, because My grace turns away from them to humble souls" (*Diary* 1602).

Mary, our Blessed Mother, also taught Sister Faustina about humility:

> "Don't do anything to defend yourself; bear everything with humility. God will defend you" (*Diary* 786).

In describing the new congregation of sisters Mary said:

"I desire that each one distinguish her-
self by the following virtues: humility and
meekness; chastity, and love of God and
neighbor, compassion and mercy" (*Diary*
1244).

Mary invited Sister Faustina to be her special
daughter and imitate her in her own virtues:

"I desire, my dearly beloved daughter,
that you practice the three virtues that
are dearest to me—and most pleasing to
God. The first is humility, humility, and
once again humility; the second virtue,
purity; and the third virtue, love of God.
As my daughter you must especially radiate these virtues" (*Diary* 1415).

Humility, humility, humility—the rock foundation of the spiritual life, the special characteristic of Mary that drew down the word of God!
She wanted Sister Faustina to share in that same
humility.

Mary continued to instruct Sister Faustina in
the interior life:

"The soul's true greatness is in loving
God and in humbling oneself in His presence, completely believing oneself to be
nothing, because the Lord is great. But
He is well-pleased only with the humble; He always opposes the proud" (*Diary*
1711).

These instructions of Mary to Sister Faustina are a profound lesson directed to each of us as well. Mary wants you and me to be her special children by sharing in her humility.

Sister Faustina learned the lesson of humility well, and she reflected on it in her writing:

> I came to know the greatness of the majesty of Jesus and at the same time, His great humbling of Himself (*Diary* 757).

> Jesus gave me to know the depth of His meekness and humility, and to understand that *He clearly demanded the same of me* (*Diary* 758).

> Oh my Jesus, nothing is better for the soul than humiliations. In contempt is the secret of happiness. . . . If there is a truly happy soul on earth, it can only be a truly humble soul. . . . A humble soul does not trust itself, but places all its confidence in God. . . (*Diary* 593).

> I will spend this Advent in accordance with the directions of the Mother of God in meekness and humility (*Diary* 792).

> The humility of love of the Immaculate Virgin penetrated my soul. The more I imitate the Mother of God, the more deeply I get to know God (*Diary* 843).

> The Lord delights in humble souls. The more a soul humbles itself, the greater the kindness with which the Lord approaches it (*Diary* 1092).

O humility, lovely flower, I see how few souls possess you. Is it because you are so beautiful and at the same time so difficult to attain? O yes, it is both the one and the other. . . . Now I understand why there are so few saints; it is because so few souls are deeply humble (*Diary* 1306).

I never cringe before anyone. I can't bear flattery, for humility is nothing but the truth. There is no cringing in true humility. . . . Jesus gave me to know that humility is only the truth (*Diary* 1502-1503).

Humility, humility and again humility—the truth on which our spiritual life is built.

10. TRUST In The Lord

January 12, 1989

May the merciful Lord bless you with His gift of trust.

What's it all about?

When fears of unknown or known origins, anxieties and confusion, and resentments all converge at once, we can easily ask ourselves this question. "What *IS* it all about?" And then add to it the worries over family and finances and mix in strained relations with those at work, and frustration with our jobs. Then top it off with sickness! It is then we scream out, "Lord what is it all about? Help! Mercy!"

It is then we need to try to listen to the silent voice of God deep within our hearts pleading with us, crying out like a voice in the desert, "TRUST ME! TRUST ME!" God speaks very loudly, but his language is silence! (Diary 888). His most common words to us are "Do not be afraid. I am with you. Trust Me." It is a phrase that is often found in the Sacred Scriptures because it is so fundamental and so much needed.

Trust in the Lord is what it is all about. Trust is the humble and free exercise of our free will, submitting our will to the will of God. Trust is a concrete and practical way to practice humility. Trust is most pleasing to God and the lack of trust is very displeasing to God as we can read repeatedly in the diary of Sister Faustina.

Trust is relying on God as the giver of all good gifts and the provider of all our needs. Trust is a way to proclaim the truth that God is God and creator and cares for me. Trust is a way to live humbly because it acknowledges that all I have is given and to be given as gift to others.

The prayer "Jesus I trust in You!" is a response to the question "What's it all about?" . . . It's all about trusting in Jesus, Who is the way, the truth and the life. In proclaiming "Jesus I trust in You," I proclaim Jesus as the source of all grace and light in the midst of my darkness. This proclamation reaches out and beyond the cloud of fears and anxieties within and around me. It is a battle cry that pierces the gloom, paying no attention to it, but paying attention only to the victory already won in Heaven so that the victory may be ours on earth. The cry of "Jesus I trust in You," is an effective plea for the coming of the kingdom where Jesus reigns, to the glory of the Father. It is a cry of victory over the works of the evil one. Our profession "Jesus I trust in You," proclaims "the kingdom, the power, and the glory are yours now and forever."

Trust in the Lord opens the flood gates of God's mercy upon us. God just can't resist the humbly, trusting soul and He floods it with His love (cf. Diary of Sister Faustina).

It seems that the Lord so desires our trust of Him that He arranges the circumstances of our lives that we must trust Him. He so loves us and respects our free will, that He wants us to exercise that gift fully and freely by trust—and He gives us plenty of opportunities each day to trust Him! We grow in trust by the practice of trust, over and over again.

So what's it all about?

Trust!

11. "This Is My Body, Which Will Be Given For You"

January 13, 1989

May the merciful Lord fill you with all His gifts.

Here at the residence, my room is directly under the Blessed Sacrament chapel. It is a reminder of the humble presence of the humble Lord. The "humble presence of the Lord" is another way of answering that perplexing question "What's it all about?"

The silent, invisible, hidden and humble presence of the Lord in the Eucharist confronts us in a most subtle way. He waits for us in patience, waiting for our hearts to be open to receive His love in this humble gift. He waits for our surrender, for our love, for our adoration; for our free and humble response of Thanksgiving to this gift of Himself.

It is a humble gift—totally given, to be totally received and consumed in order to transform us into His body. It is a gift totally offered to the Father waiting for our love and sufferings to be united to His, that His mercy may flow out on us and the whole world.

It is the most humble of all gifts. What more could the Lord do for us without violating our precious freedom? How humble can He get? Becoming our food; totally given to us that we might receive and be changed! All this that He might give us a living example of humility.

His life from beginning to end was a life of humble service and obedience to the Father's will: He came to do the Father's will (*Heb.* 10:7); he was born of a woman (*Gal.* 4:4), a man like us in all things but sin (*Heb.* 4:15). He emptied Himself in humble submission to death, death on a cross (*Phil.* 2:7-8); He was buried in a tomb of stone (*Jn.* 19:42), and in all this He loved us to the utmost (*Jn.* 13:1) showing His humility by washing the feet of His disciples (*Jn.* 13:5) and then giving Himself as food to remain with us:

> This is My body, which will be given for you; do this in memory of Me. And likewise the cup after they had eaten saying, this cup is the new covenant in My blood, which will be shed for us (*Lk.* 22:19-20).

Jesus gave us His body broken and blood poured out—now risen—as the seal of the new covenant of mercy. His complete and perfect act of humility cries out to us to receive it, and to follow in His footsteps, to be partners of Christ (cf. *Heb.* 3:14) in this work of mercy. The great mystery (the great plan of God for our salvation), is that He calls us to share with Him in this work of Mercy as His partners! Now He wants us to receive all and give all in humility. He wants us to be His body, bringing His mercy to a most needy world.

He wants us to be "Living Eucharist!"—totally given, broken and poured out for the salvation of souls. He wants us to "radiate mercy" like the Eucharist. That's what it is all about!

Without Him, we can do nothing (cf. *Jn.* 15:5). Yet we can do all things in Him who strengthens us (cf. *Phil.* 4:13), strengthening us with the bread of life and the cup of eternal salvation, to do the work of salvation.

What a "miracle of mercy" (*Diary of Sister Faustina* 1489) we have in our midst! What a challenge to humbly receive humility itself, and be transformed into His body, His partners!

What a privilege we have to come into His humble, silent presence and be radiated, so that we might radiate mercy.

May the merciful and humble Lord strengthen you to be Eucharist.

12. Mary, Mother, Model and Queen

January 14, 1989

May you be blessed with Mary's presence.

Mary as mother is the perfect model of our response to "What it's all about." Mary is our model of humble submission to the will of God. By her "yes" she became mother of mercy (*Lk.* 1:26-38), Jesus Christ, mercy incarnate. She is the model of mercy, receiving all mercy and giving us mercy itself. She proclaimed God's mercy to all generations (cf. *Lk.* 1:50). She responded with mercy to the young couple of Cana avoiding embarrassment and initiating the public ministry of Jesus (cf. *Jn.* 2:1-11); she stood with a silent "yes" at the cross as the fountain of mercy was opened for us by a lance (cf. *Jn.* 19:25-37). She prepared the apostles and disciples to yield to the Holy Spirit at Pentecost (cf. *Acts* 1:14).

Now as queen in Heaven, she continues her role as mother of mercy for all the church (cf. *Lumen Gentium-VIII*). As queen she is "mediatrix of mercy" preparing us for the second coming of Jesus (cf. John Paul II, *Mother of the Redeemer* #44).

Mary is the preeminent model of how to respond to God's plan to have mercy on all (cf.

Rom. 11:32). Now, as our mother and queen, she wants to prepare us to imitate her as she imitated her son Christ Jesus (cf. *1 Cor.* 11:1), that we too be channels of His mercy to the world. This is a great work, and it is a lifetime journey to follow in the steps of Jesus as Mary did—but this is what it's all about.

It is a lifetime journey, a journey of suffering, sorrow, and pain. Yet it can be a journey of trust and joy as well because it has a meaning, a value, and a heavenly goal. Our journey is a journey to the cross of Jesus, with Mary, to become Eucharist! It is journey to become the body and blood of Christ, totally given and poured out as channels of His mercy on us and the whole world. What a fantastic journey! And Mary is there to help us as mother and all powerful queen.

At the cross, through the words of a dying Jesus, Mary's role of mother of the Son of God was extended to all of the disciples:

> Woman, behold your son.
> Son, behold your mother (*Jn.* 19:25-27).

Through John the beloved disciple, we were all present. Now we need to personally ratify and accept this gift of Mary as our mother. This is what consecration to Mary is about. It is allowing Mary to fulfill the dying command of Jesus to take "the beloved disciple" as her son and it is fulfilling the command to take Mary as our

Mother, in order that she may offer us to the Holy One as holy (cf. John Paul II, "Fatima Homily," May 13, 1982). Her role as Mother is to bring us to the source of mercy, the pierced side of Jesus, in order that we may become holy in the Holy One by becoming the body and blood of Christ—the Eucharist.

In short, consecration to Mary is consecration to be Eucharist! By consecration to Mary, we allow her to help us in our journey to the cross of Jesus in order to become her children, her body given, her blood poured out, in Jesus. Like no priest, she can say of Jesus, "This is my body given for you. This is my blood poured out for you" (Archbishop F.J. Sheean).

Consecrating *the world* to the Immaculate Heart of Mary means drawing near, through the mother's intercession, to the Fountain of Life that sprang from Golgatha. It means returning beneath the cross of the Son... to the pierced Heart of the Savior. It means bringing the world back to the very source of its Redemption (John Paul II, "Fatima Homily," May 13, 1982).

What a magnificent description of what it's all about! Consecrating the world to the Father through Mary. "For their sake I consecrate myself...that they may be one as we are one" (cf. *Jn.* 17:19-21).

13. Entering Into The Great Circle

January 16, 1989

Peace!

How do we respond to this persistent question: "What's it all about?" How do we respond according to God's plan for us? We respond by entering the great circle of mercy and humility.

There are a variety of ways of entering this great circle as we mentioned in our letter of January 6th, and the first and most important one is Baptism. Our faith in Jesus Christ is sealed by the Holy Spirit as we enter into the regenerating waters of Baptism. We enter into the death and resurrection of Jesus, the great circle of mercy and humility. We are born anew as sons and daughters of the Father. But there is more, so much more.

Our entrance into the great circle deepens as we follow Christ's example of mercy, being merciful to others as He is merciful, doing whatever we can to help those in need. In our striving to be as merciful as our heavenly Father (cf. *Lk.* 6:36), we live out the beatitude: "Blessed are the merciful for they shall obtain mercy" (*Mt.* 5:7).

Like Jesus, our humble service is a channel of mercy, whether it is washing dishes and laundry, or dirty feet. In being merciful, we obtain mercy for ourselves and others. In being humble, we extend our channels of mercy, since only the humble can receive mercy.

We enter more deeply into the great circle by trusting like Jesus. He trusted in the Father, knowing that even if He dies the Father would raise Him up. By trusting, He received mercy; He was raised from the dead. He answered His own question to Martha:

> I am the resurrection and the life; whoever believes in Me, even if he dies, will live; and everyone who lives and believes in Me will never die. Do you believe this? (*Jn.* 11:25-26).

When we proclaim "Jesus I trust in You," we profess our faith in the resurrection of Jesus, and ours, and enter more fully into the great circle.

We can also enter more deeply into the great circle, by prayer, by asking for the gift of God. Our prayers can be simple, often repeated cries of the heart: "Father, Your will be done." "Jesus, mercy." "Come Holy Spirit." These simple and sincere cries are powerful ways of responding to the various situations around us. These short prayers keep the heart's fire burning with God's presence and mercy.

In all this, Mary is our mother and model. She takes us into the depths of mercy and humility, preparing us to be Eucharist—totally received, totally given.

Over the years words that I heard in my heart

during special retreats have been like battle cries
for me—encouraging, reminding, strengthening.

From the Ignatius spiritual exercises (January,
1974):

> Take My hand and walk in the light,
> in simple faith, as a child, as a Son. Re-
> joice always. Pray without ceasing. "In
> all things give thanks for this is the will
> in Christ Jesus regarding you all" (cf. *1
> Thess.* 5:16-18).

From the time of solitude (December 25, 1985):

> To please Me, be present to Me with
> your heart in the heart of Mary, trusting,
> rejoicing. Radiate mercy and Eucharist.
> Jesus, Mercy! Come, Holy Spirit! Come,
> Lord Jesus!

From the time in solitude (December 8, 1988):

> Walk in humility. Trusting! Rejoicing!

May these reflections on how to enter more
fully into the great circle of mercy and humility
be an encouragement to you on how to respond
to the persistent question:

"What's it all about?!"

14. Reflections on Humility: HT₃

March 14, 1989

Humility continues to be a growing concern for me. I see its importance, and I also see my need of it.

Why humility? Because humility is the response to the need of our times and is a response that has been needed throughout the ages. The sin of Lucifer was pride, a rebellious "I will not serve!" The sin of Adam and Eve was also pride, "We can be like God!" The sin of the Jewish leaders who condemned Jesus was self-righteous pride. The great sin our age is the rebellious independence from God, a practical atheism that seeks self and self-fulfillment. I'm convinced of the need of humility, but questions immediately arise. What is humility?

In the novitiate of the Basilian Fathers in 1946, I strongly sensed from reading and from teachings that spiritual pride was the worst possible sin of the spiritual life, but I do not remember that spiritual pride was ever defined. I assumed it meant not talking about yourself, and as a result I fell into spiritual pride because I didn't acknowledge God's gifts in my life.

So I've decided for myself, to re-define humility as "boasting." Since not talking about myself led to spiritual pride then boasting might have

49

the deserved effect, as long as it was a two-fold boasting. On one hand it must be a boasting of God's mighty power and on the other hand a boasting of my weakness and misery. Sounds like Mary our Blessed Mother, and St. Paul! This definition of humility is based on the traditional description of humility as truth. I am creature and sinner, but He is Lord and giver.

I've continued to search for a clearer and fuller definition of humility. These past weeks, I've come up with a chemical formula, a biochemical flashback: HT_3. Humility can be described with three "T''s: Truth, Totality, and Transparency.

TRUTH: Humility is the truth and the truth is that we are creatures of God, made in His image and likeness. We are His children. It is a big fat lie to listen to words that would say to us that we are no good, or that we have no value. The truth is that we are made to reflect God by our reason, our freedom, our unity and love. Of course we are sinners; but Christ Jesus is our Savior, and a bigger Savior than we are a sinner.

TOTALITY: Humility is the openness to receiving totally and giving totally. It is all a gift. We have received everything from God as gift and we pass it on to others in love, mercy and service as a way of returning it all to God. "The gift you have received, give as a gift" (*Mt.* 10:8). In this dimension of humility, we reflect who God is. He is humility itself, totally giving all to His Son and the Son receives all and returns it in the Holy Spirit. In Christ Jesus, the Father has given us all.

TRANSPARENCY: Humility is being transparent to

God's presence and grace; His presence radiated to others when there is an obstacle of self and sin. A humble person radiates God's merciful love because in seeing Him, we can see the Lord. The Holy Spirit orders our lives to be like stained glass windows, letting His light shine through.

This formula, HT$_3$ can be tested against some beautiful and powerful examples: Jesus, the Eucharist, and Mary.

JESUS is truth. He said of Himself, "I am the way, the truth, and the life" (*Jn.* 14:5). He is the Son of the Father and the Son of Mary, and He knows it and claims it. He is totally given, even to death on the cross for our salvation. He totally received mercy in the resurrection. He is transparent. Seeing Jesus, we see the Father (cf. *Jn.* 14:8).

EUCHARIST is the truth incarnate. It is the Body and Blood, Soul and Divinity of Our Lord Jesus Christ. It is total gift, totally given to be received. How humble can God get? It is transparent. It radiates to those with eyes of faith.

MARY is the model of humility. Her statement to St. Bernadette at Lourdes is a perfect statement of humility. "I am the Immaculate Conception" is the truth—she is the spouse of the Holy Spirit, the eternal, uncreated Immaculate Conception. The Immaculate Conception is total gift, since she didn't exist until it happened. Because of her Immaculate Conception, she is sinless and transparent to God. Seeing Mary, we see Jesus.

Truth, totality, transparency do give a more complete picture of humility, but the real issue is: "How do I grow in humility?"

Three actions working in consort can zero in on humility, like three points used in surveying. Surrendering to God's will, invoking the Holy Spirit, and rejoicing in our humiliations are common to all of us, and are growth patterns in humility.

SURRENDERING TO GOD'S WILL: "Fiat!" The "Fiat" of Jesus (*Heb.* 10:7) and Mary (*Lk.* 1:38) are a model for us. They surrendered their wills, their plans to God's, that His will be done. This is what Jesus taught us in the Our Father (*Mt.* 6:10). This is the prayer of Jesus in the Garden of Olives as He humbled Himself to do His Father's will (*Mt.* 26:42) in entering the passion.

The surrendering of our free will to the will of the Father is the greatest exercise of our free will, and the way to reach real freedom (*Jn.* 8:32 and 36).

This act of the will is the foundation of all prayer. It is the greatest act of love because we allow Him to love us by having His will accomplished in us.

INVOKING THE HOLY SPIRIT: "Veni Sancti spiritus!" Inviting the Holy Spirit to come and take possession and control of our lives is to ask Him to purify us, to sanctify us, and so make us transparent to His radiant presence. We invite the Holy Spirit to remove every obstacle that obstructs His radiance.

REJOICING IN HUMILIATIONS: "Gaudete." Rejoicing in the Lord is probably the hardest of the three actions but it makes us grow the quickest. Jesus rejoiced in seeing Satan falling from his place of pride (cf. *Lk*. 10:17-23). "For the sake of the joy that lay before Him He endured the cross, heedless of its shame" (*Heb*. 12:2).

In his 30 day spiritual exercise, St. Ignatius of Loyola gives us the meditation on the two standards: That Satan's way is "riches and honors that lead to pride," and is opposed by Christ's way of "poverty, and humiliations that lead to humility." He points out that with the grace of God, but only under the direction of a spiritual advisor, you may even beg for humiliations in order to grow in humility! What a grace! It is a prayer that the Lord answers immediately, because He so loves humility.

My experience is that we have more than enough humiliations each day to practice our rejoicing. Humiliations are God's way to make us grow:

> My sons, do not disdain the discipline of the Lord nor lose heart when He reproves you;
>
> For whom the Lord loves, He disciplines; He scourges every son He receives.
>
> . . .God does so for our true profit, that we may have His holiness. . .(*Heb*. 12:5-13).

"Fiat, Veni, Gaudete." A three step prayer for all circumstances. Three steps in the dance of life.

The mystic Sister Faustina Kowalska (1905-1938) left us a clear example of humility. In her diary she records the words of our Lady to her asking for humility:

> I desire, my dearly beloved daughter, that you practice the three virtues that are dearest to me—and most pleasing to God. The first is humility, humility, and once again humility; the second virtue, purity [of intention]; the third virtue, love of God. As my daughter, you must especially radiate these virtues (*Diary* 1415).

Sister Faustina lived a humble life and was aware of the need of humility. She comments on the fact that there are so few saints because there are few who are deeply humble (cf. *Diary* 1306). Her advice to grow in humility is to meditate on the passion of Christ (*Diary* 267) and to rejoice at humiliation (*Diary* 270).

Rejoicing in humiliation is certainly the hardest on our self-will and pride. It hurts to live this way, but is there another way that is effective, efficient and trustworthy? This is the way the Father chose for Jesus and Mary. Who am I not to follow the Father's way for me? Personally, I know the way, but it still hurts. It is painful—but does that really matter?

15. A Visual Parable of God's Humility and Mercy

March 15, 1989
Rome, Italy

From my window on the third floor of the Teutonic College within the Vatican, again I am watching the pilgrims streaming into the papal audience hall. It is only 9 o'clock, Wednesday morning, and the audience begins at 11:00 a.m. but the early arrivers are anxious about having a front row or aisle seat. Each Wednesday morning, these past two months, crowds up to 10,000 people have been streaming by under my window and then streaming out again about 12:15 to 12:30. On Saturday mornings there are special audiences for villages and language groups, and there was one for families of missionaries. Some have come with banners, village bands, colorful costumes, all with an expectancy.

People of all nations, age, color, and creed are anxious to see the Holy Father, and be in his presence. The speeches are long and they don't always understand them, but they bear patiently for the moment for their group to be recognized, or by chance to be close enough to touch him. All receive his blessing. All see him.

At this moment, a fife and wooden flute orchestra is playing, awaiting its turn to enter the hall. They are right from an Italian village, in native dress.

People, people, people! These 10,000 today are only a small fraction of the 5,000,000,000 on this planet earth, each created by God as individuals reflecting His image and likeness, each loved by God, each in need of His mercy. Each are free to know, to love and to serve God. Each one's freedom is respected by the Lord, Who, in His humility will not violate their freedom.

Last week, I was especially moved to see this humble respect of God toward us lived out below my window. It was after 11:00 a.m. The crowds had entered the hall and I could hear the Holy Father addressing the audience. Outside at the main entrance stood the Swiss guard in his multicolored uniform, and one elderly man who was watching a young boy, about seven or eight years old. No one else was in the square.

The little boy was crying with his thumb in his mouth. He didn't want to go in. He ran away a few yards and pouted. The elderly man, I assumed to be his grandfather, went out to him, embraced him, talked to him, but again he ran away still further. The grandfather was perplexed. What could he do? He so wanted the lad to see the Holy Father and he himself wanted to see him as well. Again he went out to the boy, wiped his tears with his own handkerchief, kissed him, talked to him, but to no avail. This time the grandfather pretended to enter the audience hall, hoping the boy would follow suit. Shortly he returned to try again. What could he do!

I was struck by this living and visual parable.

The grandfather didn't want to violate the freedom of the boy, yet he wanted something very good and precious for him. He was in a dilemma. Finally he took the boy by the hand, led him out the gate and they went home. They did not see the Holy Father. The grandfather was saddened, but in his dignity, he respected the boy's freedom. He really loved him in a humble way.

How humble God is toward us. How He respects our freedom, even tolerates the abuse of it when we sin and turn away from Him and cry and suck our thumbs. God continues to persue us, to coax us and pour out His merciful love upon us so that we might turn to Him, accept what He has prepared for us and find true freedom. He really is the "hound of Heaven."

Lord continue to reach out to the thousands streaming by. Each and every person needs to know Your loving mercy.

NOTE:
The letter of March 14th and 15th are further reflections on humility and were written during a subbatical at the Teutonic College in the Vatican City.

16. Epilogue:
The Counter-Sign To Our Age

January 22, 1990

So what's it all about?

Our free and humble submission to the Lord! It is to trust Him because He is mercy and humility itself. It is to thank Him for everything, because all is a gift given in love.

I see more and more clearly that our humble submission to the Lord is THE counter-sign to our age. Ours is an age of independence, rebellion, sophistication, self-fulfillment and pleasure seeking, and it doesn't want to hear about humble submission. And yet, this is what the Lord asks and expects of us because He loves us so much and wants to use us to bring about His kingdom.

For a number of years I've been searching for such a sign that could be an obvious contradiction to the secular media and its blurring out of the messages of Our Lord. Could it be radical poverty? Could it be our freely setting aside competition, advancement, spectator sports, the mass media? Is it seeking to live Christian community? Yes, it is all these things and more. It needs to be a radical lifestyle and attitude that God is God, and that He is the giver of all good gifts. It needs to be a way of life that gives God the glory and

honor in all, and for all. It needs to be a way
of living that allows the Lord to express His extreme humility and mercy in using us to continue the work of His Redemptive Incarnation.

In essence then, this means that I must live
like Mary, live her "yes," her "Fiat," and live
her "Magnificat." It means that I must give thanks
to the Lord for the mighty things He does in
and through His lowly servants, and it means
I cooperate with Him and give Him all glory and
honor in proclaiming His kingdom.

Yes, THE counter-sign to our age is humble
submission and rejoicing with thanksgiving in
all things. This is the sign of Mary, the sign that
appears in the Book of Revelation, the great sign
in the heavens (*Rev.* 12:1).

The ultimate victory is given to the "woman
and her seed" (*Gen.* 3:15), Jesus Christ, and the
rest of her offspring, those who keep God's Com-
mandments and bear witness to Jesus (*Rev.* 12:17).

> Lord, in this our age, send Your Holy
> Spirit that we may live the Fiat of Mary
> and rejoice in thanksgiving as we live her
> Magnificat.

This way of living a Marian life would be a
transparent life—transparent to the Lord's mercy
and thus radiating His mercy to others. It would
be a way of living the Eucharist, the proof of
God's love, blessed by Him, but hidden, then
broken in order to be given to others for their
salvation.

Mary, intercede with your Son as you did at Cana, that we may receive the gift of the Spirit and be transformed into living Eucharist, radiating His mercy, and truly be THE counter-sign to our age.

What's it all about?
To be living Eucharist!
To radiate His mercy!
To live the Magnificat!

FAITH PUBLISHING COMPANY is a publisher and distributor of religious books. It is committed to the orthodoxy of the Roman Catholic Church, and the Pope as the successor to the Apostles, and St. Peter.

Faith Publishing Company publishes books that reflect these values and other non-religious books that adhere to the principles of faith and trust in our Creator, and that promote peace and love in a violent world.

Faith Publishing Company also distributes books for the Riehle Foundation including a wide variety of titles on the apparitions in Medjugorje, Yugoslavia. We welcome your inquiries.

Fr. George W. Kosicki has also authored an additional book published by Faith Publishing Company, *ICONS OF MERCY.* It includes a series of meditations on the spiritual needs of the Church and its shepherds, which apply to the laity as well.

For additional copies of this book, or *ICONS OF MERCY*, send your request to:

 FAITH PUBLISHING COMPANY
P.O. Box 237
Milford, OH 45150

What's It All About: $3.00 per copy

Icons of Mercy: $6.00 per copy